DR. TOAD'S
SHORT BOOK FOR A LONG MEMORY

DR. TOAD'S
SHORT BOOK FOR A LONG MEMORY

Improve Your Recall and Retention with Simple Strategies Anyone Can Use

JEFFREY TOLSTAD MD

Wellness Writers Press

WELLNESS WRITERS PRESS

An imprint of Pure Ink Press

Paperback ISBN: 979-8-9912047-5-0
Ebook ISBN: 979-8-9912047-6-7

Illustrated by Marlon at GetYourBookIllustrations

wellnesswriterspress.com
jeffreytolstad.com

CONTENTS

INTRODUCTION

Should I Be Worried About My Memory?

**How to Know if You Have a Serious Problem or
You're Simply Forgetting Things the Way Everyone Does**

No matter your age, you've undoubtedly had moments when you blanked out on someone's name or a word that you KNOW you know. A simple word. An obvious word. Yet, it's not coming to your mind. In your sudden silence, anxiety rears its ugly head, and you are left awkwardly trying to describe the word and regretting that you ever started talking.

"Ahhh... that bubbly stuff that sits on top of beer. YOU know."

"You mean *'foam'?*" asks your friend in a worried tone.

Or you compose a text, an email, or write a paper for an assignment, and you suddenly get stuck on coming up with the exact word that conveys the most accurate meaning you want. Again, you KNOW that word and have used it dozens of times in the past. *Gah! Why can't I think of it now?!*

You do a quick online search: What is that word for... the aircraft thing that looks like a huge American football that floats slowly around in the sky... has a company name on it... *blimp!* Of course!

Why do these things happen? Should you be alarmed that you're experiencing an early onset of dementia? Should you swear off red meat and video games until your brain fog lifts?

If you are over 50 and you forget a word or phrase, you will probably experience some amount of anxiety about being early on the road to dementia. If you are younger than 50 and you get stuck on recalling something, you will probably feel anxiety about appearing unintelligent, or at least not as smart as you think you should be.

Solution: Make fun of yourself, no matter your age, to provide yourself a cushion of time:

"What's that word for... *'the thingy with the whatsus'?*"

Joke about how tired or sleep-deprived you are, or how you must have left half your brain in bed when you got up this morning. Use self-deprecating humor to diffuse your anxiety and give your subconscious mind the time it needs to recall that for which you are searching.

In most cases, that word on the tip of your tongue is elusive because your mind is distracted by something simple: A new post on Instagram. A reply text from your friend.

The realization that your favorite TV show or podcast is about to start. The surprise entrance into the room by your grandma Blanche and her heavy perfume. The stress you feel by the report you haven't started that your boss expects tomorrow morning.

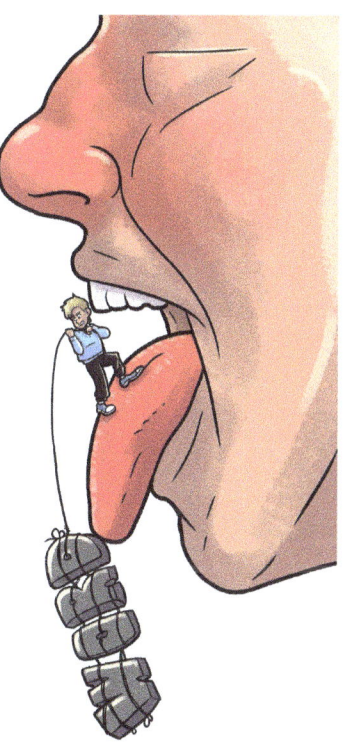

It can be and usually is any number of simple to complex thoughts, sights, sounds, and even smells that hijack your mind's attention for the moment. Your mind is constantly "multi-tasking," which is really a misnomer because studies show you cannot focus well on more than one thing at a time.[1] What self-described "excellent multi-taskers" really do is shift from focusing on one thing to the next at warp speed. It's called "switch tasking."

With all this switching going on, it's understandable that a word or phrase might fall down between the floorboards of your mind and disappear for the moment.

What to do? Again, smile broadly, make a joke about how you just realized you left a load of towels in the washer, and give yourself a few moments by distracting your audience. During a moment of self-deprecating distraction ("I can't believe I can't think of this word... did you see the Lakers game last night?"), your mind, one hopes, will retrieve that elusive little rascal. Just give your subconscious a few seconds to send it up to your conscious mind.

The fact that *you realize* you forgot a word is reassuring. It's when you *don't* realize you're addressing your wife by another name or that you neglected to put on socks this morning that you should start to worry. If you're putting the milk carton back in the microwave and your underpants in the fridge, people will notice and advise you to get help.

(Speaking of distraction, *patter* is the term used by magicians and politicians that refers to things they say that cause you to look in one direction while they expertly reach from another direction into your pocket to grab their rabbit or your wallet.)

Sorry to tell you, there is no magic pill, ritual, or exotic fruit that will guarantee to elevate your brain power. (Although there ARE a lot of people who want to sell you such things with enticing promises of success and "this week only" discounts.) We will further explore this topic in our Day 7 Chapter. It's natural for you to want a quick fix without any work involved. I've found that most things of value in life come with the price of some significant personal effort.

Worldwide, it's estimated that about 10 percent of the population over age 65 has a diagnosis of "dementia."[2] That number goes up to 35 percent for people in their nineties.[3] Yikes! There are things you'll learn in this book that will help you reverse transient memory loss and also mild cognitive impairment (MCI), or at least delay their progression. You will also learn how to find that elusive tip-of-the-tongue word or phrase, names of friends, your grocery list, and much more. "Use it or lose it" applies here.

You may have heard how one climbs a mountain. "One step at a time." You will learn how to link one bit of information to another to assist your retrieval of that info. The links on your chain can be literally dozens long. And these links, or associations, can be of various types, depending on what works best for you. (See Day 1 Chapter, on Primary Learning Styles.)

Research over decades by many diligent experts has revealed insights and suggestions that might help you improve your brain and memory health. There are plenty of studies published and varying points of view. I suggest you do an online search for specific topics and methods you wish to understand better.

I always tell my patients, "Listen to your body. It will tell you what to eat, drink, and do to be merry." Read Martha Morris's book, *Diet for the Mind* for solid, honest answers about which foods will help and which will hurt your brain. (See References at the end of this book.)

Putting in a little work now to master a few simple memory skills will save you a lot of work later.

I have never been labeled a "genius," and indeed am not one. (Just ask my children.) Getting new information deep down into your brain isn't so much a matter of being super smart but of utilizing the proper techniques that help ensure efficient success. You can do this!

HOW TO USE THIS BOOK

Scan the Table of Contents and see if any particular topic grabs your attention and addresses a problem that especially bothers you. You don't have to read the chapters in order, but you will get the most out of this book if you read them all. There are seven days in a week, so there are seven chapters, one for each day of this short journey to improve your recall and retention. You will amaze your friends and family with your improved memory powers. Have fun with this!

DAY 1

Can't We Just Skip to the Techniques?

Your Primary Learning Style and Why It's Important

Recalling something you memorized is much easier if you used your primary learning style when you first got hold of the material. You remember things even better when you use more than one style. There are a few different ways of categorizing learning styles, depending on who does the categorizing. Some researchers creatively describe as many as eight different styles, such as "The Linguistic Learner," "The Naturalist Learner," "The Kinesthetic Learner," "The Logical (Mathematical) Learner," and "The Social Interpersonal Learner," and more.[4] You likely already know your primary learning style.

For our purposes, we shall use the "KISS" principle* and ask you to consider just these three:

Sight

Also called "Spatial" learning, using either reading or watching something to understand it. You easily "see" images in your mind.

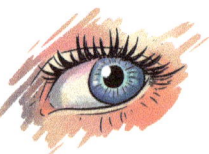

Auditory

Taking in information by listening and/or speaking out loud. "Hearing" sounds, musical tones, or words in your mind.

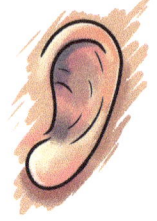

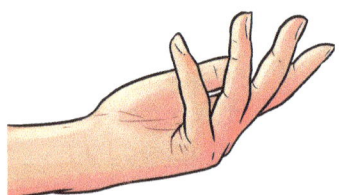

Tactile

Also called "Kinesthetic" learning, by physically performing a skill or task—the "hands-on" person.

(Add in **Smell** and **Taste**, which go together nicely, as fourth and fifth supplemental styles to these three, and you're off to the races.)

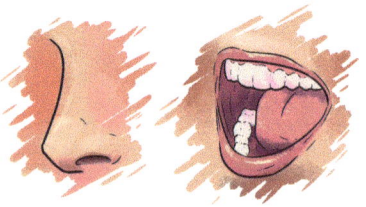

The percentage of people who are primary learners in one style or another varies with which researcher you read. It seems that about 65 percent of people are Visual Learners, about 30 percent are Auditory Learners, and only about 5 percent are people who learn by participating in some manual activity (Tactile Learners).[5]

*The "KISS Principle" = Keep It Simple, Student (We try to keep things polite around here.)

Using more than one style when you first learn something will help cement it more firmly in your memory for later recall. Preparing a meal is a great example. Read the recipe out loud to yourself or your indifferent cat while you use your hands to prepare the ingredients and smell the various spices or sauces as you mix and cook. Taste test along the way. *Bingo!* Betcha next time you won't even need to read the recipe.

You normally form memories in three quick steps.

First, your *senses* (sight, sound, touch, taste, and smell) are presented with information from the world outside you.

Second, if you determine that information is important, you pay attention to it by *focusing* on it, so that it then enters into your short-term memory (STM). Studies show you can hold up to six or seven different pieces of information at one time before that short-term part of your memory system overloads and one or more items spill out and disappear.[6]

Third, if you decide some of this information is important enough that you need to remember it later, then you move it into your long-term memory (LTM). You do this by repeating words and phrases silently or out loud, forming visual images or auditory tones in your mind that *link the new information to associated information* already in your long-term memory from all of your life experiences so far. This process usually happens at lightning speed, so you are mostly unaware of it. The ease with which you form new memories and reinforce existing memories is called *neuroplasticity.* Think of this as describing how flexible the parts of your brain are that handle your memories.

Why does this work? Because, in very general terms (and here comes some memory science stuff), you form memories primarily using two distinct parts of your brain. Your *hippocampus* forms what's called "logical memory," which includes numbers, facts, lists, and so forth. Your *amygdala* is used to form emotional, feeling-based memories.

For example, you may have associated a very peaceful, happy feeling with the smell of freshly baked bread or your mother's homemade baklava. By employing vivid, even outlandish imagery while you purposely form a memory of a name, object, or place, you engage both your hippocampus and your amygdala to deeply ingrain that memory. These brain centers were designed to work best together to create memories. This exaggerated imagery technique may seem bizarre or even childish to you at first, but that's exactly why it works! We will get into this more later on.

You will learn to apply some amusing techniques in this book that will end up making your long-term memory implanting process much more efficient and complete than it has ever been for you before.

A *mnemonic* (from the Greek word "mnemon" meaning "mindful") refers to a collection of techniques that employ clever and creative associations to help recall information. In medical school, I was taught an ancient mnemonic about the twelve cranial nerves. "On old Olympus' towering tops, a Finn and German viewed some hops." The first letter of each word in this sentence stands for the first letter of a cranial nerve. I will spare you the anatomy lesson of naming the nerves.

An *acronym* is a set of letters that stands for words. For example, "FBI" stands for "Federal Bureau of Investigation." "ADD" stands for "Attention Deficit Disorder." "DOA" stands for "Dead on Arrival." "CMO" stands for "Chief Marketing (or Medical) Officer." People who post frequently on social media have perfected the art of the acronym to a high degree: "BTW" = "by the way." "TLTR" = "too long to read." "TTYL" = "talk to you later." "LMAO" = (I'll let you look that one up yourself if you don't already know it.)

An *alliteration* is when you use two or more words that have the same letter or sound in adjacent or closely spaced words. For example, "red ripe raspberries," or the very old and well-known, "Peter Piper picked a peck of pickled peppers." Songwriters and other musicians often use alliteration for titles and lyrics: "Born on the Bayou" by Creedence Clearwater Revival, "Cat's in the Cradle" by Harry Chapin, and the Joni Mitchell lyric, "They paved paradise and put up a parking lot." These titles and lyrics are easy to remember because of the similar-sounding words, which help market and sell these songs.

Take your mountain of school or office work you need to memorize and arrange it into one or more of these literary devices that make some sense to you. Create a narrative story employing as many memory tricks and techniques as you can. If you're creative enough, you could make parts of the story rhyme, use alliteration, and include acronyms and mnemonics.

If your primary learning style is auditory, then saying or singing your material out loud will further embed it into your memory. Link it all in the correct order with the Roman Room technique. (See Day 4 Chapter.) By the time you're done, you'll know your material so well and be so impressed with your memory creation that you may want to share it with class or office mates.

How You Forget to Remember

If you do not review new information after it is first presented, you will forget about 50 percent of it within an hour, about 70 percent within forty-eight hours, and 90 percent within a week. As you may have experienced when you walked out of a lecture at school or work, you felt that you understood what was presented and would easily remember it because it was, *in that moment*, readily recallable. This is a deceptive feeling! Just one hour later, you likely won't do well on a test of your memory of that material. At eight hours, the majority of the information will be forgotten. The rate of loss slows down after that.

The implications are obvious: If you want to beat the "Forgetting Curve," you need to review new information as soon as you can after it is presented, then review again a little after that initial review, then later again for a third review.[7] Alternatively, reviewing information in little bits for ten to twenty minutes at a time over the week following the initial presentation will help you more easily retain for the long term what you want to recall later.

Paul Pimsleur was a researcher in the field of languages called "linguistics" at Ohio State University and UCLA. He discovered through years of research that we humans can learn and remember foreign languages if new words and phrases are *repeated* at an optimum frequency and sequence. Auditory learners will especially excel using Pimsleur's method.

I learned Spanish, French, and Norwegian to varying degrees of proficiency using the "Pimsleur" approach. His system illustrates the importance of repetition soon after learning, with decreasing frequency of repetition as time goes on and the information gets more deeply embedded. He created an ideal system for learning and retaining foreign languages based on his research.

But repetitive review is not the only thing you need to do. As you will learn in this book, when you want to remember something that's important, you will *associate* it with things you already know—things you've accumulated during the course of your life's experiences. Scott Young, in his book *Learn More, Study Less!,* says, "Instead of trying to pound information into your brain with the hopes it will simply fall out when you need it, holistic learning is the process of weaving the knowledge you are learning into everything you already understand."[8] This is what I mean by associating new info with things you already have sitting in your brain.

DAY 2

What Was Your Name Again?

A Foolproof Way to Remember People's Names

You're walking down the aisle of your neighborhood market, thinking about how you wish you had not left your grocery list at home. Then you see her coming right toward you. She doesn't see you yet, but you know she soon will, and you are blanking on her name.

You KNOW her. Is she the wife of that guy who talked too loudly at Cicero's Italian Bistro last week? Is she someone in your office? OMG—do you know someone who is dating her? You frantically try to find the *context* in your memory for where you've seen her.

Gah! She just looked me in the eye and smiled. No escape now!

What WILL you do?

You could blurt out, "Hey there, *you.* How's it going?" (Lame, but it might get you by just this one time.) Or, you could completely skip any greeting and ask her with alarm in your voice if she's heard it's supposed to rain this afternoon. (Now she'll *know* you forgot her name. It's a bright, sunny day outside. Doh!)

The key to avoiding this embarrassing event would have been to *prepare ahead of time.* That, of course, doesn't help you now, but should motivate you for the future. The next time you are with someone—even someone you know well—focus your attention on his or her face. (No scary staring, though!) What feature stands out? A squinty eye? A unique nose? Prominent lips? Big hair? High cheekbones? Or perhaps no feature stands out, and they have what's called a "boxer's face," where everything is flat (which in itself stands out). Look at photos of people you know and whose names you must remember next time you see them.

NAME TECHNIQUE: Take a facial feature and exaggerate it in your mind to the point of absurdity. Take it into cartoon land. Next, link that exaggerated visual to their name. Sound out their name silently in your mind, and out loud as well, if that won't make you feel awkward. Vigorously employ your imagination. Here are some examples to help you get the hang of this technique.

"Elaine Stewart": Looking at her, you notice that Elaine has long hair that's parted in the middle. Imagine her hair on either side of her face as the side boundaries to a *lane* on a road. Now visualize an enormous, towering letter *E* on top of a very bright and colorful painting of a bowl of *stew* at the end of the road. An "E"-labelled painting of a bowl of stew at the end of a "lane" helps you remember "Elaine Stewart."

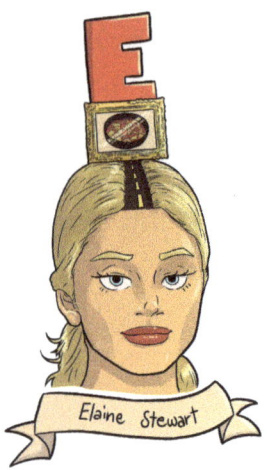

Elaine Stewart

"Robin Austen": You notice she has naturally curly hair. Now, imagine a red-breasted *robin* nested in that bush of hair. The robin sits guardedly on a pile of little blue eggs in the nest it's built. You think, "Wow, that's pretty *awesome!*" Voila: Robin Awesome becomes Robin Austen.

Robin Austen

One more. "Scott Campbell": You know where I'm going with this one, right? You see that Scott has a moustache. Even if he doesn't, imagine a moustache rapidly growing out of his upper lip and encircling his waist to create a *Scottish* kilt. You picture Scott in his kilt, standing next to a roaring *camp*fire, which is next to a massive *bell* suspended from a wooden beam. Scott grabs hold of the camp bell pull, yanks it down, and the bell peals loudly, "Soup's ready!"

Scott Campbell

Salespeople have a trick they commonly use when meeting new potential customers. They look a person in the eye and ask what their name is while shaking their hand (or bowing). The name is repeated out loud two times. You should do the same. Go even further. Ask them about the spelling of their name. "Is that 'Lauren' with an 'o' or 'au'?" "Is that Michele with one 'l' or two?" When they answer, picture that spelling in your mind and, of course, exaggerate it and associate it with something they are wearing or their hair color, age, or any feature that stands out. If you have your phone or a pen and paper with you, write it down. They will be flattered if you think their name is so important that you took the time to do so.

You might ask them if they have a business or personal card. In some cultures, when two people exchange such cards, they both take a moment to study that card carefully. It is considered disrespectful to simply take someone's card and immediately put it in your pocket as we do in the U.S. If a person hands you a card, read it out loud, and then take a pen or pencil and write the date of your meeting on the back. Then make a comment about his or her line of work, company or product name, or work address, as you say the name again. The point is to use as many of your senses as you can (remember "learning styles"?) to embed that name in your memory.

If the person's name is unusual or doesn't immediately cause you to think of something familiar, then change their name in your mind so it sounds close to something that *is* familiar.

Again, I know this process seems weird, but it WORKS, so who cares how strange it is? (As you'll find out, it's usually best to *not* describe your visuals to anyone else, especially those who are the subjects of your memory creations. They can—and should—get personal. Even outlandish or silly. That's why you remember them so well!)

Before you attend an event where you know there will be many people whose names you want to recall, prepare ahead of time by writing a list of as many of those names as you can. Next, mentally create associated images with each one. Vivid, ridiculous images with colorful animation and action. When you get to the event, you will astound yourself by how easily this technique works as each name pops into your conscious mind as you greet everyone. Please exercise self-control to keep from laughing out loud as you greet people and visualize your associated image. You will have a LOT of fun using this technique.

With practice, you will no doubt become an expert at this. Can you imagine how valuable remembering names could be at your school, workplace, or social group?

For practice, look at these pictures of people and their names for one to two minutes. Use your full imagination to take those names into fantasy land. Look at their unique, distinguishing features. Now, cover the names with a sheet of paper or some other object and see how many you remember using the techniques you've just learned.

Jackson Jones

Yasmin Ahmadi

Luna Flores

Maddy Iversen

Bhola Rai

Ovie Adewumi

DAY 3

Our Sales Increased This Year By...uh...a LOT!

Remembering Statistics, Dates, and Other Numbers

A lot of people can recall names and images more easily than they can remember numbers, facts, and figures. That's because numbers are essentially abstract marks on a page, whereas names and objects have a more concrete visual image associated with them, so you can more easily link with facts and images you already have in your long-term memory.

A quick and easy way to remember numbers is to group them into smaller bits. Recall that your short-term memory can hold up to six or seven bits of info before you max out.

You probably know your Social Security number without having to look it up. I bet you memorized the nine numbers in three groups:

123-45-6789

The same goes for phone numbers:

123-456-7890

Take a number you need to remember, like 4506284. Break it up into two or three groups of numbers: 450-62-84. Or, 4506-284. You'll see how easy this works if you try it.

If you can associate a small group of numbers with something in your life, then so much the better. For example, let's again use the number 4506284. Perhaps you are age 45, and you realize that you have 6 children. O my, that's a lot of children! A street address of 284 may be somewhere you frequently shop, like your market.

You think, "I'm *45* and *O* my! I have *6* children who eat like horses. I'd better go to the market, which is at *284* Main Street." If you can find something to relate your numbers to, then you more easily lock them into your long-term memory.

Some people include a sing-song addition to their groupings, or "sounds" in their minds with musical notes rising up, then down. "123, climb a tree. 456, pick up sticks. 789, I can rhyme." Or: "450, go with the flow. 628, 4 heaven's sake." You get the idea.

Besides grouping, there is a more complex approach to remembering numbers. This may not be for everyone. Read what comes next and decide if you are willing to invest the time and effort required to make this system work for you. It just might be worth it.

There is what's called the "Mnemonic Peg System," or "Numeric Peg System,"[9] where you rhyme a number with a word: 1 = "bun," 2 = "shoe," 3 = "tree," and so on. These are examples of simple rhyming, but now we will add a visual element for each single digit.

Picture the digit itself as marked on a page, then match it to an image of something that looks similar to the digit. You will be best served if you take the time to create your own mental visual system of images linked to digits because you can best "see" what a digit looks like to you. Once you have created your own digital visual system, use these images to create a vivid sequence of links in the correct order.

Here is my own digital visual system, which I have used many times. (The more you use something like this, the easier it becomes.)

HERO

SUN

SHOE

TREE

DOOR

HIVE

STICKS

HEAVEN

GATE

VINE

For example, if sales in your company are up 27 percent over last year, and you want to remember this number, you could visualize a shoe floating up to your version of heaven.

DAY 4

I Sure Wish I Hadn't Forgotten My Shopping List

Easily Remember To-Do Lists and Presentation Points

This technique is especially good for visual style learners and for remembering lists of unrelated items, such as a grocery shopping list. Or for recalling linked items, such as major points in a presentation you will give.

Long, long ago in a faraway land... in Rome, actually, a couple of thousand years back, public orators like Cicero developed a way to memorize key points in their very long speeches. You can use this same technique today and be absolutely amazed at how much you will remember.

ROMAN ROOM TECHNIQUE: Also called the "Mind Palace," "Memory Palace," or "Method of Loci."[10] (This last one sounds like the title of a science fiction novel!) There are whole books available just on this one technique. You start by closing your eyes and visualizing a room you're familiar with, typically in your home. *It should be a room that you know very well,* where you can "see" in your mind every table, lampstand, wall hanging, window, and door. It could also be your workspace or office.

Start by picking up to four different objects in the room, on which you will mentally "place" or link just one item you want to remember. Use your by-now well-developed imagination to enlarge and creatively enhance the object you wish to remember.

For example, let's say you have a list of four things you need to buy at a grocery store:

Eggs

Bread

Coffee

Apples

In your "Room," visualize the lampstand that is next to the couch. Imagine a carton of a dozen eggs sitting on top of the lampstand. Then imagine the carton pops open by itself and tips on its side. Then all the eggs spill out onto the carpet. Next, visualize the carpet getting wet with raw eggs and "see" a loaf of bread on that carpet. That loaf is soaking up the eggs. Now look up at the couch that's near the bread loaf. Imagine there is a huge can of coffee that takes up all the sitting space on the couch cushions. Now look at the bookshelf behind

34

the couch and the jumbo coffee can and "see" the shelves filled with apples instead of books. You have just linked one item to another, then to another in sequence. You will remember this sequence when you start with the first item, which will lead your mind to the second item, then to the third item, and so on, until your list is complete.

Now, let's say you have more than four items on your list. How about ten? Twenty? You will need more objects or sometimes more rooms with their own objects to "walk" into for longer lists. Your Roman Room will become your "Roman Home." Here's how you add them:

Imagine yourself coming home. In your mind, open the front door and walk into the entryway. Now, continue to walk through your house on a route that you will always take each time you imagine doing this technique. Let's say you go from the entryway to your living room. From the living room (where your carpet smells like spilled eggs—are you ever going to clean that mess up?), you pass the kitchen on your way to your bedroom.

For each room, starting with your entryway, visualize up to four objects that are permanently there. Use each of these objects as places upon which you put items on your list. *What matters is the ORDER* in which you mentally walk through your home, so that the correct order of items will then automatically appear during your walk. One item is linked, or associated, with the next, then the next, and so forth.

What also matters with this technique is how creatively you visualize each item and where it is placed. You "look" in your mind around the various rooms on your path through your home and "see" the items on each object. Eventually, when you get really good at this technique, you can even mentally open drawers in a dresser or doors in a cupboard in rooms to place even more items. TRY THIS. It's been working for centuries!

If you have a list of a dozen or more items to remember, you can also determine if there is a way to group words into general categories that make sense. You might have a "liquids" group, an "automobile and truck" group, a "work tool" or "kitchen appliance" group, and so forth. Once you have a group, you can then place that group somewhere in your Roman Memory Room or Home.

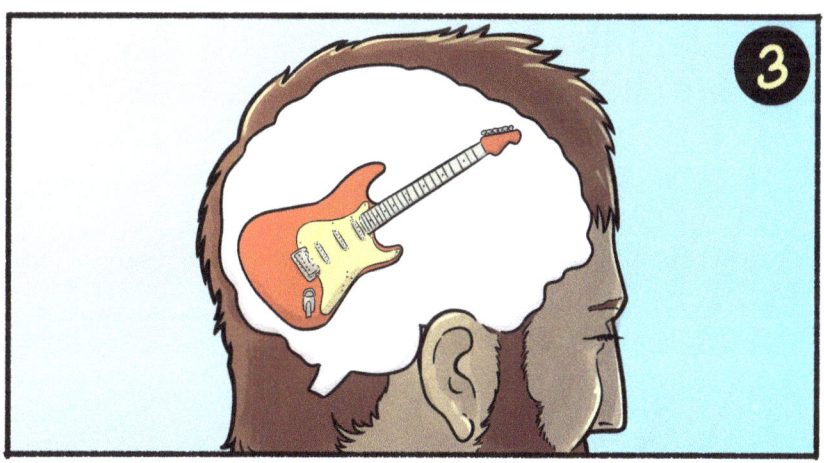

VERY IMPORTANT: You should *physically walk* through whatever place you're using for this technique, such as your home, school, or office, at least once every day, if possible, in the exact same path you imagined for your Roman Room technique. Burn into your mind every physical object present along that path. If you are out of town, away from home or office, repeat this walk *in your mind* at least once every day.

With practice, you will be able to add more than four objects in each room on which you can place more items. If you don't visualize your Roman Room pathway regularly, then your view of your rooms will fade. Police detectives are trained to enter a room or crime scene and notice fine details that most of us overlook. You can train yourself to the same degree as a detective, so you notice things no one else does and remember them.

VARIATION – MAKE YOUR BODY YOUR "ROMAN ROOM":

You might prefer to use your body instead of a set of rooms to help you remember lists. You start with your hair and associate the first list item, then move down to your nose for the second item, your mouth for the third, your chin for the fourth, your chest for the fifth, and so on down to your toes if your list is that long.

DAY 5

Oh No, I Lost My Phone! Have You Seen My Car Keys?

Create Your Personal "Mind Vault" that Holds the Locations of Your Most Essential, Must-Have Items

You swear you left your mobile phone right here on the kitchen table, but nooooo. It's NOT there now. Take a moment to backtrack in your mind to the last place you remember seeing it.

Instead of losing your phone, it might be your car keys, wallet, purse, medications, or other item of importance. I'm confident you recognize this all-too-familiar scene. Knowing the location of items of daily importance for when they are needed is essential. You need a way to create a *Mind Vault* in your brain, like your own personal bank safe that protects these items so you can access them dependably at the right moment.

Start by carefully selecting fixed places to put specific items every time you finish using them. Every time! For example, you might have a small table by the inside of your front door. When you arrive home after school or work or wherever else you've been, make it a habit to ALWAYS place your set of keys and purse on that small table. Always. If you need one of these items later, be sure to put it back in the same place after you're done using it! I know this sounds as if I am encouraging you to become overly focused, but this is nothing more than using *consistency* to your advantage. (Plus, it will encourage you to keep your home nice and tidy.)

Perhaps you take your shoes off after you enter your home. Then you usually walk in and sit down on your couch to catch up on the news with your roommate, spouse, child, or the news anchor on your television. You still have your phone with you, right? Choose a spot to ALWAYS place your phone that's convenient for you and out of the way of anyone else. Coffee table? Top of the TV? Arm of your couch? Or keep it in your purse or pants pocket?

For medications that you need to take every day, use plastic pill boxes of various sizes that are organized by day of the week and even by "a.m." and "p.m." Search online or at your local pharmacy to find one that makes sense to you and meets your needs. If you have pills you take every morning when you wake up, put them in your bathroom in a place where you'll see them when you walk to your toilet.

Perhaps you take more pills or supplements before going to bed at night. Put them in a pill box on your nightstand so you can't miss seeing it when you start to climb into bed. Place a water bottle next to your pill box so you can take those pills right there without missing a beat. Pleasant dreams!

Choosing specific places gets you into the habit of associating each important item with ONE location. Make the extra effort to do this even though you may be tempted to just toss everything on the chair because you're exhausted from a long day.

I promise the extra energy expended will be worth it later when you avoid wasting time looking for an important item.

MIND VAULT TECHNIQUE: (Similar principle to the Roman Room) Once you have the locations of your essential items firmly set, find a place without distractions to think about (ponder) each item with its linked location. See an item in your mind as you get up in the morning and move from room to room and place to place. Note the location of each item. See in your mind that radiantly colorful pill box jumping up and down on your bathroom sink. Make your nearby toilet seat flap up and down, "Hello!" See your phone grow to ten times its usual size, until it dwarfs the now-tiny cushion it sits on. Visualize your set of keys spinning rapidly on that small entry table. By now, you realize the Mind Vault is a variation of the Roman Room technique. You're getting the hang of this memory thing!

How about remembering something that's presented to you *unexpectedly?* Let's imagine that you are out to dinner with some friends. One of them mentions that a local art museum will open an exhibit in five days, and it sounds fascinating. You want to remember to attend this exhibit, but are afraid you'll forget because you're just so darn busy.

You most likely have a smartphone with a calendar or notebook app, and so you enter "art exhibit" with an alert to remind you of it. But if your phone just died and there's no way to plug it in to charge it at the moment, do not worry. By now, you know how to use association to help you remember things. Simply put the event and date temporarily in a "safety deposit box" you visualize, which you then place on the first fixed location in your Mind Vault until you need to "open" it.

Though not in any peer-reviewed scientific studies that I know of, there is a collection of "folk customs" that some people think truly work. For example, clenching your dominant-side fist while you are memorizing something and then relaxing the dominant fist while clenching your non-dominant fist with the same information, alternating between the two sides several times back and forth, seems to improve accuracy in about 10 percent of those studied.[11] This method engages the right and left halves of your brain for better recall later. Others say chewing gum vigorously while focusing on the information you want to remember will increase recall by about 25 percent for the first fifteen to twenty minutes.[12]

Another technique is to look from side to side by moving your eyes without moving your head while thinking of the desired memory. Or crossing your arms, placing your hands on the opposite forearm, and tapping first with your right hand and then with your left, back and forth, back and forth, for about thirty to sixty seconds. All these types of techniques involve a theory that *uniting a physical action with mental learning* increases interactive neural activity between the two brain hemispheres. This is the idea behind a form of psychotherapy called "eye movement desensitization and reprocessing" (EMDR).[13] And this technique works, according to much research. (This is not to be confused with "tapping for relief of anxiety," an emotional therapeutic technique.[14])

In the Day 7 Chapter, we will discuss this theory as it applies to dancing and other activities that enhance memory and stave off cognitive decline.

DAY 6

Now, What Did I Come In Here For?

**How to Remember What You are Looking For and
How to Retrieve That Word on the Tip of Your Tongue**

You've likely experienced this: You are in a room you just entered to fetch something, and suddenly, you forget what it was you went in there to get. Frustrating, right? Even alarming. This happens to both young and old, as well as those in between. It happens because our chain of associated thoughts, which includes the desired item, is broken. What to do?

Stop and stand still for a moment. Ask yourself out loud, "Now, what did I come in here for?" Mentally, or physically if you need to, backtrack to the room you just vacated to the point where you can recall what you decided you needed to fetch. Remembering your train of thought might bring back the memory of why you left that room and what you came into this one to get. Oh yes! Your glasses! So you can read about the fun memory game your friend brought over to share with you. Of course!

You think, "How could I have forgotten such a simple thing like my eyeglasses?!" Again, sequences of thoughts occur in a *context:* where you are, with whom, and your emotional state, as one

thought links to the next and the next and the next until you decide you need to temporarily leave that context to obtain something to add to the situation. Like your eyeglasses.

Maybe you were in the first room chatting with someone at the moment you decided to leave, and that person might recall what you said you needed to get. Since this commonly happens to everyone at some point, there's no need to be embarrassed. Again, use self-deprecating humor. It never fails. "I was transported to this room from the Mothership so you and I could enjoy chatting. Then I left you to get something, but I've come back now because I forgot why I left. Do you recall why I said I was leaving?"

You blank on the object you decided to get because you removed yourself from the original context of your train of thought. So, get back into that context. Relax, don't rush, and the memory will emerge from your subconscious mind to the surface.

This experience is similar to the elusive word on the tip of your tongue we discussed in the Introduction. To further help retrieve your elusive word, try audibly describing it as an intentional part of your story: "That white, bubbly, frothy...*foam!*" Stumbling upon a word that starts with the letter "f" (frothy) automatically links to the word you want that also starts with "f" (foam). Yay! You got lucky on that one. Alternatively, you might try to mimic holding an invisible full beer mug and swirling it to the point of spilling the... *foam*. Voila! You'll quickly find out what method works best for you.

If you can visualize an object but can't remember its name, then you might use the "Alphabet Search."

ALPHABET SEARCH TECHNIQUE: While you were giving a brilliant description of the Belgian Beer Industry, you got stuck on the word *foam* and it all went south. Distraction was the culprit. When you don't want to ask for help from a worried friend, suspicious spouse, or embarrassed child, try using the "Alphabet Search."

This technique's title means exactly what it says: *Sound out words in your head* starting with the letter "A," then "B," and work your way rapidly all the way to "Z," if necessary, and hope to land on your desired word.

For example, a visiting friend invites you to go into town. You realize you need an article of clothing hanging in your hall closet before you leave your apartment.

You tell her, "I'd love to go. Just let me get my..."

Then you totally blank out on the name of what you need to get. You can mentally see this familiar article of clothing hanging in your closet. You're too excited by the thought of finally getting out of your place and having some fun with your friend. *What* is that thing called? You use it all the time. Seconds are ticking by, and your friend is beginning to wonder why you're silently standing still with a vacant stare and open mouth.

Here's what to do: Mentally, start with the letter "A," and go through the alphabet in rapid-fire speed to jog that word loose. *Ankle weights?* No. *Boxers?* No. *Camisole?* No. *Drugs?* No! *Envelopes?* No. *Frying pan?* In my closet? Are you kidding me? *Gun?* Nope. *Hockey stick?* No. *Intimate apparel?* Not tonight. *Jacket?* BINGO! This process took all of maybe two to three seconds.

"... jacket and we can leave."

If this Alphabet Search doesn't work, then switch to describing what your word represents, telling your friend how you're SO embarrassed you can't think of the word. Use gestures and pantomime putting it on, if you have to. She's a good friend, so she'll probably be amused. Even if she gets worried that you're mentally slipping, by now it has become a battle: It's win by remembering that infuriating word refusing to come forth to your mind, or lose face and worry about an early onset of cognitive decline, besides missing an evening out with your friend.

Always remember that *the word is in there*, in your brain, somewhere. It just needs the right nudge to come out of hiding. Once found, it's a good idea to purposely use the word as often as you can for the next several days, saying it out loud to form a lock on it for future use. "Why are you wearing your jacket to bed, Mom? It's 80 degrees in here."

DAY 7

The Other Stuff

How Diet and Exercise Can Improve Your Brain's Health

Supplements such as Ginkgo Biloba, Vitamin D3, Resveratrol, coconut oil, creatine, and methylene blue, among many others, have anecdotal and correlative evidence of improving memory and cognition. While a full review is beyond the scope of this short book, there are double-blind, peer-reviewed studies on some of these and many other supplements and compounds.[15]

Anecdotal cases are not the "scientific method." Correlation does not equal causation. Meaning, just because people think their memory improves after taking a certain supplement doesn't mean that the improvement was achieved because of that specific supplement. The "placebo effect" might have been a contributing factor, for example. I am all for taking supplements, as long as you've first checked with your healthcare provider, you are confident in the purity and quality of the product, and you know exactly why you are taking it. See what happens.

Uncle Bill knows he's overweight and out of shape. He knows he's not as mentally sharp as he was during his career as an accountant. He took an early retirement when it was offered by his company. He's unhappy with his life, even though he's retired. His "golden years" seem more like a rusty iron prison.

"I'm too young to be this old," he laments. Bill knows, deep down in a place he doesn't want to visit, that his current condition is his own fault. Habits usually first modeled by parents, followed by a lifetime of daily repetition, will produce either healthy or premature aging. An online search about this broad topic yields thousands of studies that confirm this principle. Overall physical health includes brain health, which affects the mind's ability to learn, understand, and remember.

Sure, have a glass of wine at night if that's your thing, but not the whole bottle. It's okay to have a piece of your birthday cake, just don't finish off the rest of it after everyone else has had a slice and left. Sorry to be blunt, but you already know this. The older I get, the more the ancient admonition of "All things in moderation" is proven correct. Most scholars think it was Hippocrates, the father of medicine in ancient Greece, who first gave that advice. Maybe it was Aristotle. Who knows? It's sound advice that many people have followed for millennia.

Much research has concluded that moderate to brisk *walking* (jogging or running is not required, though you will burn more calories) for a minimum of thirty minutes for five days each week will make a significant improvement in your overall cardiovascular health.[16] Your brain needs adequate blood flow to stay in top condition. Walking is the most efficient way to circulate body fluids, like blood and lymph, more than jogging or any other activity. Start walking for fifteen minutes, then turn around and walk back to where you started. Use your by-now prodigious memory powers to recall, "thirty minutes times five days" to help you get into this walking habit. See the References section at the end for "Midwestern Doctor" and his writings on Substack.

May I Have This Dance?

Secret Ways to Keep Your Brain Working at Its Best

Some years ago, I met an 85-year-old gentleman who was a member of a ballroom dancing group. He and his fellow seniors met twice each week to learn new moves and practice old ones. This man told me that dancing was his "secret weapon to prevent getting Alzheimer's."

Research supports his theory.[17] If you have done any dancing with a partner, you know that one partner has to lead and the other has to follow. Otherwise, there's a chaotic, stumbling mess. In ballroom dancing styles, the couples hold each other in what's called "the frame," with arms and hands positioned so that, with often only a light push or pull, the follower knows what the leader wants to do next.

The leader has to think three or four moves ahead so that the dance keeps flowing smoothly. Plus, he needs to be constantly aware of other couples dancing nearby to avoid a collision. The follower must tune in to the potential signals the leader may send. The couple's brains are highly engaged with their bodies during dancing. This applies to *any* type of dancing, by the way, but those dances with one or more partners, such as line, square, or ballroom dancing, give your brain the best workout.

This same principle of connecting mind to body movement applies to activities similar to dancing, such as yoga and tai chi, as well as playing a musical instrument or video game. Learning a foreign language involves activating and using a part of your brain that may have been dormant for years.

About 40 percent of Americans forget or misplace something at least every week.[18] Stress and an unbalanced work-life are major reasons Gen Zs and Millennials forget things, sometimes more often than their grandparents.[19] People over age 55 experience one or more memory lapses without an underlying medical condition at about the same frequency as younger people.[20] "Senior" citizens, defined as "those over age 65" (whatever happened to "60 is the new 40"? I was counting on that!), more commonly forget names compared to younger people.[21] Why? Too many accumulated life experiences crowding the mind? Distractions in the immediate environment? Maybe you have your own theories... A fun and helpful article in the *New York Post* several years ago is recommended for your enlightenment.[22]

"Dementia" is defined as a persistent disorder of thinking due to actual brain injury or disease that causes loss of memory. It usually includes personality changes and an impaired ability to reason logically. Between transient memory loss and true dementia is a condition called mild cognitive impairment (MCI), which affects short-term memory.[23] ("Mild" doesn't sound all that bad, right?)

True dementia conditions (there are quite a few types besides "Alzheimer's," by the way—look up Robin Williams and "Lewy Body" dementia, for example) usually leave long-term memories intact. That's why Grandpa Bob can tell you all about his days as a boy on the farm in North Dakota in great detail, yet forgets he ate lunch ten minutes ago.

CONCLUSION

Most people today, and I bet that includes you, would say they feel "stress." Many of us experience moments of anxiety from feeling overwhelmed with workloads and responsibilities. Chronic feelings of anxiety and mental burdens activate biochemical processes that lead to high cholesterol and triglycerides (fat in your blood), which can clog up your arteries and decrease blood flow to critical parts of your body, like your heart and your brain. There are loads of books about stress-reducing methods, and I urge you to look seriously into reducing the overall stress in your life as much as is doable.

I encourage you to walk out of a life of stress and forgetfulness and onto a sandy, peaceful beach of order, sharp thinking, and reliable memory.

I hope the memory techniques in this book will help you reduce some of the burden you feel to keep many, many things in your memory. You will feel more in control of your life and experience lower stress levels by consolidating information into groups and "packages" that are readily retrievable from your Roman Room and Mind Vault.

ABOUT THE AUTHOR

Jeffrey Tolstad, MD, MMM, is a physician with decades of experience in both pediatric and adult anesthesiology. His career began with a foundation in psychology from the University of Southern California and grew through medical training at George Washington University, and beyond, where he developed practical strategies for learning and memory that supported his professional growth. More than forty years later, he earned a master's degree in business back at USC, where he went on to serve as Senior Associate Dean.

Beyond medicine, Jeffrey has explored diverse fields— including entrepreneurial business ventures, community theater, screenwriting, and the hospitality industry—bringing a broad perspective to his work. His writing seamlessly blends insights from medicine, leadership, and personal experience with practical science, offering readers tools to strengthen their memory, improve their health, and enhance overall well-being. His books provide clear, fun and actionable guidance for navigating everyday challenges and living more fully.

REFERENCES

1. www.dakim.com

   A brain "exercise" website primarily for seniors and those who care for them.

2. *Born on a Blue Day* by Daniel Tammet, 2006, by Free Press.

   A fascinating book, *Born on a Blue Day* was written and published in 2006 by Daniel Tammet, a young man with the diagnosis of "savant syndrome," a form of autism. He could perform complex calculations in his mind. Daniel was able to clearly describe how his mind works: He "sees" a rolling landscape in his mind, for example, where numbers are specific colors, shapes, and textures in a certain order. He is unique for being someone who has a significant autistic disorder while being able to vividly and understandably explain to others what is going on in his mind. He uses his powerful, creative mind to recall things of importance by associating a fact with a vivid visual mental image or auditory sound.

3. *Diet for the Mind* by Dr. Martha Clare Morris, 2017, by Little, Brown and Company.

   A terrific science-based resource that includes many recipes for a healthy brain.

4. www.memorydynamics.com

   My own journey down memory lane began by taking a course titled "Arthur Bornstein's Miracle Memory Course" in West Los Angeles way back in the 1970s. Mr. Bornstein was a wonderful teacher, making our work with him fun, entertaining, and best of all, improving our memories to an astounding degree. (Go to this Memory Dynamics website to see more of the Bornstein family's superb courses.) By the end of a week's worth of classes, all thirty of us students could perform all sorts of memory skills, recalling facts, numbers, names, long lists of random words, and other feats. We amazed ourselves!

5. Numerous books and publications on brain health by Gary Small. He works at the UCLA Longevity Center. www.semel. ucla.edu/longevity

6. *The Memory Book: The Classic Guide to Improving Your Memory at Work, at School, and at Play,* by Harry Lorayne and Jerry Lucas, 1996, by Ballantine Books. One of the original best sellers with lots of details and advice for your further education.

7. Alzheimer's Orange County association in southern CA.

8. www.braintraining101.com

    This fun website is full of resources to help you maintain and improve your brain health, cognitive function, and memory.

9. A Midwestern Doctor: The Forgotten Side of Medicine.

    You can access his writings on Substack (https://substack. com/@amidwesterndoctor). He describes a variety of often complex medical and health topics in easy-to-understand, "average person" language.

BIBLIOGRAPHY

1   Napier, Nancy K. "The Myth of Multitasking." *Psychology Today*, May 12, 2014. https://www.psychologytoday.com/us/blog/creativity-without-borders/201405/the-myth-of-multitasking.

2   Nichols, Emma, et al. "Estimation of the Global Prevalence of Dementia in 2019 and Forecasted Prevalence in 2050: An Analysis for the Global Burden of Disease Study 2019." *The Lancet Public Health* 7, no. 2 (2022): 102–125. https://doi.org/10.1016/S2468-2667(21)00249-8.

3   Manly, Jennifer. "One in 10 Older Americans Has Dementia." *Columbia University Irving Medical Center*, October 24, 2022. https://www.cuimc.columbia.edu/news/one-10-older-americans-has-dementia.

4   Davis, Tchiki. "8 Types of Learners: Definitions, Examples, and Learning Strategies." *The Berkeley Well-Being Institute.* Accessed September 4, 2025. https://www.berkeleywellbeing.com/types-of-learners.html.

5   Nikolaroza. "Statistics, Facts and Trends on Different Learning Styles 2025." *Nikolaroza*, March 3, 2025. https://nikolaroza.com/statistics-on-learning-styles-facts-data/.

6   Miller, George A. "The Magical Number Seven, Plus or Minus Two: Some Limits on Our Capacity for Processing Information." *Psychological Review* 63, no. 2 (1956): 81–97. https://doi.org/10.1037/h0043158.

7   Ebbinghaus, Hermann. *Memory: A Contribution to Experimental Psychology.* Translated by Henry A. Ruger and Clara E. Bussenius. New York: Teachers College, Columbia University, 1913.

8   Young, Scott H. *Learn More, Study Less!* 2nd ed. 2015. https://www.scotthyoung.com/learnmorestudyless/default.html.

9   "Mnemonic Peg System." *Wikipedia.* Last modified August 4, 2025. https://en.wikipedia.org/wiki/Mnemonic_peg_system.

10   "Roman Room System." *Art of Memory*. Last modified April 14, 2023. https://artofmemory.com/blog/roman-rooms/.

11   Propper, Ruth E., Sarah E. McGraw, Todd T. Brunye, and Michael Weiss. "Getting a Grip on Memory: Unilateral Hand Clenching Alters Episodic Recall." *PLOS ONE* 8, no. 4 (April 24, 2013): e62474. https://doi.org/10.1371/journal.pone.0062474.

12   Onyper, Serge V., Timothy L. Carr, John S. Farrar, and Brittney R. Floyd. "Cognitive Advantages of Chewing Gum: Now You See Them, Now You Don't." *Appetite* 57, no. 3 (2011): 665–68. https://doi.org/10.1016/j.appet.2011.05.313.

13   Cleveland Clinic. "EMDR Therapy: What It Is, Procedure and Effectiveness." Last modified September 4, 2025. https://my.clevelandclinic.org/health/treatments/22641-emdr-therapy.

14   Ortner, Nick. "Tapping Therapy and EMDR: Understanding How These Powerful Techniques Work Together." *The Tapping Solution*. Last modified September 4, 2025. https://www.thetappingsolution.com/blog/tapping-therapy-emdr/.

15   Jafari, Reza S., and Valiollah Behrouz. "Nordic Diet and Its Benefits in Neurological Function: A Systematic Review of Observational and Intervention Studies." *Frontiers in Nutrition* 10 (2023): Article 1215358. https://doi.org/10.3389/fnut.2023.1215358.

16   Mayo Clinic Staff. "Walking: Trim Your Waistline, Improve Your Health." *Mayo Clinic*. Last modified September 4, 2025. https://www.mayoclinic.org/healthy-lifestyle/fitness/in-depth/walking/art-20046261.

17   Gajjar, Amyn. "Dementia and the Benefits of Dance." *Dr. Amyn Gajjar*, June 19, 2017. https://dramygajjar.com/dementia-and-the-benefits-of-dance/.

18   Hargis, M. B. "Remembering Proper Names as a Potential Exception to the Tip-of-the-Tongue Phenomenon." *Journal of Experimental Psychology: Learning, Memory, and Cognition* 46, no. 5 (2020): 825–34. https://doi.org/10.1037/xlm0000782.

19   Gallup. "Generation Disconnected: Data on Gen Z in the Workplace." *Gallup Workplace* (blog), November 11, 2022. https://www.gallup.com/workplace/404693/generation-disconnected-data-gen-workplace.aspx.

20   Hargis, M. B. "Remembering Proper Names as a Potential Exception to the Tip-of-the-Tongue Phenomenon." *Journal of Experimental Psychology: Learning, Memory, and Cognition* 46, no. 5 (2020): 825–34. https://doi.org/10.1037/xlm0000782.

21   Ibid.

22   Haaland, Marie. "The Most Embarrassing Thing to Forget, According to Research." *New York Post*, June 29, 2020. https://nypost.com/2020/06/29/the-most-embarrassing-thing-to-forget-according-to-research/.

23   Mayo Clinic Staff. "Mild Cognitive Impairment (MCI)." *Mayo Clinic*, September 15, 2023. https://www.mayoclinic.org/diseases-conditions/mild-cognitive-impairment/symptoms-causes/syc-20354578.